THAT WHICH APPEARS

Thomas A Clark lives in a fishing village on the east coast of Scotland. His poetry explores the landscape and culture of the highlands and islands. Numerous small books, cards and editions from his own Moschatel Press investigate ways that the presentation of poetry can inform sense and nuance. During the summer months, with the artist Laurie Clark, he runs Cairn Gallery, a space for minimal and conceptual art.

THOMAS A CLARK
that which appears

CARCANET POETRY

First published in Great Britain in 2024 by
Carcanet
Alliance House, 30 Cross Street
Manchester, M2 7AQ
www.carcanet.co.uk

A CIP catalogue record for this book is
available from the British Library.

ISBN 978 1 80017 385 9

Book design by Andrew Latimer, Carcanet
Typesetting by LiteBook Prepress Services
Printed in Great Britain by SRP Ltd, Exeter, Devon

The publisher acknowledges financial
assistance from Arts Council England.

CONTENTS

THAT WHICH APPEARS

it is early
a trickle of stones
released by light from ice
tumbles across the path

beyond the deer fence
a stag bellows
unseen in
dawn light
in the possibility
before things
find their limits

the walls of the old fort
wait
in the truce of the morning

a granite mass
inserted into granulite
with veins of pegmatite
intrusions of
felsite and porphyry

the mountains continually
crumble away
broken by the cold
into which
they lift themselves

mica flakes
sparkling in granulite
like a fossilised
memory of ice

all is explicit
accomplished
complete

the visible
is absolute
and without weight

corrie of the snows
burnt rock
surging river
hill of the stranger

in such light
one might sleep
in such cold
never wake

isolated crags
and corries do not
press down on the moor
but rise above it
in an agility of white
that converts to air

there are marks in the snow
but no paths or trails
each step sinks deeply
where bird, deer, hare
run lightly

in the silence of the birchwood
snow melting from branches

in the stillness of the birchwood
snow melting from branches

snow on moss on stone

green, ochre
russet, gold
colours refreshed
and released

wash face with snow
taste snow
clap hands in clear air

up on the ridge
surrounded by light
standing at ease
on crumbling rock

where all is so
insistently clear
it will not do

something is hidden
a premise of which
the facts are a residue

nothing coincides
with its representation
stop look wait

the visible is fragile
the call of a whimbrel
might split it apart

light comes
streaming
down into
a moment
which is all
encompassing

it is the ache
of looking
perceives
behind appearances
that which
appears

heather or ling
a roughness
covering scars

removing a stone
to alter the melody
of a mountain burn
I listen
then place
it back again

on the far
lake shore
a scree slope
rising steeply
the lake water
rippling gently
in the lee
of ruin

lichens, droppings, stones
I bend to inspect
detail in a clarity
I cannot leave

this is the gift
of the afternoon
this one moment
of stillness among
evidence of collapse

the way forward
is from side to side
leaping from rock to rock
pausing, balancing
taking off

progress is impossible
without gaps and lacunae
the steadying halts
the taking of breath
the absence of thought

ascending, descending
turning to the right
turning to the left
space opening, closing
pressure brought to bear

small continual
adjustments of the spine
the hips and shoulders
the head inclined slightly
forwards or back

in a succession of
departures and accommodations
I move through a space
that opens before me
that falls behind me

my perception of it
is discontinuous
a sampling of aspects
like the arcs and angles
of sky between branches

there is ample distance
while that which is near
in being present
exceeds itself becoming
brittle and strange

as I myself am far
from myself in
those moments in which
I am most opaque
dead bracken or rock

wind in the pines
land slipping
spawn in ditches

for shade and company
a fern by a stone

in a small hollow
out of the wind
warmth is added
to clarity

sunlight
dust and flies
in webs
among ivy

the moss on the gravestone
the waters rushing by

a few yards from water
a heron with blood on its wing
the feathers still subtle
with dusk and distance
the lines of the body
even in collapse
speak of grace and flight
the beak of direction
only the eye has lost
its concentration

an old gnarled root
dried out and dishevelled
the rope still around it
that dragged it from the ground

parting the flow
a moss-covered boulder
sprinkled with golden
alder leaves

storm driven waves
lifted as spray
over a rise to feed
weed held waters

the pondweed is held
by water that
the pondweed holds

a line of pebbles
laid out on the sand
the light falls upon
each one differently
the tide flows in around
each one differently

among green and black boulders
the slap and the break of waters

among grey and black boulders
the leap and collapse of waters

among brown and black boulders
the swell and subsidence of waters

what the wave delivers
the ebb takes back

in the grey shoreward
advance of the waves
far out a lonely
instant of grey
arrestment and enquiry

out in the wind
burning

out of the wind
glowing

a broken gate leading nowhere
mist closing every distance
water held in deep moss

mature trees spread
long branches over
an open habit
of mossed rocks
ling or heather
blaeberry and crowberry

standing dying trees
standing dead trees
fallen logs and stumps

eaten by insects
inhabited by birds
bryophytes and fungi

quiet is
replenished
growth and clearing
maintain themselves
in a steady
regeneration

where many trees
grow together
they modify
the weather

through horizontal layers
of soil, litter, shrub
the trees rise to a canopy
which is their final delay
before the breadth of the sky

a pool in the forest
a place where the stillness
looks back at itself

beneath the ripples
on the green lake
the sublucustrine
ripples of light

air is filtered
through pine needles
held by alder
scrubbed by juniper

thin frosted
birch branch
more frost
than branch

thin lichened
birch branch
more lichen
than branch

between birch and mist
an affinity

an extension
where every
direction is foiled
intention is stilled
an openness
sheltered

for one who forgets
who no longer waits
the crested tit will come
to the hanging lichen

a steady rain falling
through birch branches holding
clear rain drops

fissures in the bark
pathways for rain

the stillness is deeper
in the rain

a little stream passing
under the trees
reflecting
refracting

in darkness a light
altering in
intensity
now on and now
by a stone

in an ardour of stillness
moss on a stone

moss on the trunk
catching the light
lending to the tree
a glowing silhouette

a horizontal branch
the upper half in shadow
the lower half lichen stained
as if a light shone on the branch
upwards from the ground

as I go
through the trees
I am led
through the trees
I progress
by implication

a recess
of green
guarded
by thorns
and lit
by its own
internal light

to the side of the path
where it turns to avoid
the corner of a field
a few steps to the left
through long grass
a pool beneath an oak

sunlight continues
to warm a small
recently vacated
depression in grass

there is a flicker
in the light
where heat
rises

emptied
of content
I look
across at it

at dusk
I came down
through fields
and saw
in the remaining light
a man moving
among cattle

twilight
when all the ache
of distance
comes near

sparks rising from
a bonfire of rosewood
the air dancing

a deposit of dusk
on the eyelids, in the ears
in the mouth

between day and night
in the hollow of itself
the occasion is held

the man at the gate
the stoat, both have emptied
themselves of intention

light drains
from the glen
water batters
against rock

around a tangle of grasses
the darkness closes

in a wide
darkness
the touch
of rain

THE HUNDRED THOUSAND PLACES

once again
for the first time
morning

a sea mist closing
every distance
cliffs falling away
from the edge of a world
only half accomplished

listen
feel your way out
into what might
wave or rock
take form

you are not sure

there where you hover
over yourself
stay there

as if you were implicated
the lifting of the mist
from the water

the grey wake of a boat
unmoored at dawn

colour
the first
candour

the gorse flower
tenderness
nourished on rock
in a salt wind

primrose
of the islands
opened
by light
first primrose
of the islands

the lapwings
call to you
to confuse you

veering away
they call to you
to confuse you

a wide stretch of sand

you walk out
into space
as to
an appointment

with so much
space around you
intention
drops from you

here is where
forward momentum
runs out in
pure extension

no longer
ahead of yourself
in imagination
nor behind yourself
pushing on

you walk
above yourself
space spreading round you
the sand
bearing your weight

a path through the gold
of bird's foot trefoil
delayed by the pink
of thrift or campion

as it turns
in the long grasses
you are coloured
by events

there where
you lose yourself
brightness
takes your place

sit down on the rocks
impatience exhausted
thyme, thrift and clover
where the space is wide
hours should be wasted
thyme, thrift and clover

green islands
on blue seas
blue lochans
on green islands

drifting between
green islands
a red boat
on blue water

eight hundred
acres of heather
for the step
and the stride

on bright days
the world is brittle
the solid rock
is insubstantial

as you tread the deep
accumulations
a snipe cuts
a curve in space

between sea and sky
drifts of bugloss
a blue butterfly
lifting from the lyme grass

cormorant and herring gull
orpine and clover
sorrel and sea kale
redshank and plover

sunshine its climate
openness its aspect
detail its pleasure

the fields are drenched
in lark song
in detail
in dew

knee-deep in flowers
the red bull is lazy
muscle-bound
slightly drunk

as far as you can go
over the machair
there is only surface

it is a plane
of appearance
where nothing
is deferred

lacking depth
you walk on the richly
embroidered ground

the blue butterfly's
moment on the purple
thistle flower
is indolent

idly its hoarded
blue is unfolded
onto difference
then folded again

heard but not seen
the corncrake in the grasses
steps through fragrance

shy of exposure
seeking the shelter
of complexity and fragrance

asphodel, milkwort
eyebright, ling
the lovely particulars
brighter than their names

through crushed water-mint
through particulars you come
to a blue boat moored
beside purple vetch

if you stretch out
in the long grasses
your weight is distributed
over the headland
to rest as lightly
on the crushed grasses
as sky on sea

turning back from the sea
from margins and limits
behind yellow dune and grey dune
beyond the old hay meadows
follow your inclination
a drift of thistledown

the interior quiet
thistledown and bog cotton
a sweet scent
of cattle and wool

the place names
are exclamations
and sighs

not a stranger in the glen
without a rumour on the breeze
not a stray sheep on the hill
without word of it

along back roads
to far dwellings
single track
with pausing places
by vetch and clover

behind a straggle
of honeysuckle
the distances
laid on open
dog rose petals

through mud and manure
to hill farms
dark with neglect
a depth of fragrance
stored in the barn

at leisure a shape
lifts from rock and flaps
out over wastes
a few wing beats
taking it far

stretching inland
blackland and moorland
grassland and acid heath
a dark country
of heather and moor grass
of deer grass and moss

around the ruined
sheep folds and shielings
green islands
of sweet vernal grass
bent grass and fescue
rescue wilderness

a whim
of wind
in dry
whin thorns

a song
of wind
through bare
rib bones

whatever is lifted
by the wind is dropped
again into a calm
slightly ahead of itself

strong hill shapes
presiding over
pastoral slopes

sheep grazing
salmon in pools
of clear water

runnels of water
freshets of water
many voices

grey lichens
resting on branches
as if they had dropped

from the air

brighter than evergreen
fresh shoots on larch branches

their constancy is not
to continue in the same

but to return again
to spring, to morning
freshness and vigour

one song of water
picking up
from another

the slopes
constantly
spilling water

as you climb
it pours
around you

rushing, dashing
leaping to find
its level

stretch out
on the slope
beside water

where it leaps
headlong you resist
the inclination

there you go
but for a counter
weight or inertia

you do as you please
taking your ease
against the slope

the rock in the water
breaking the full
weight of the flow
produces melody

the rock by the water
broken by bracken
tormentil and heather
releases colour

from rock
heather
from astringency
colour

the many strands
of water are tied
in a woven braid
or plait of water
tossed in the early light

taking the slope
you glance back
at a grace or tress
of water and light

as you turn a corner
of the forest path
the face of the mountain
looms up before you

it knocks you back
for a moment
the force of it
straddling the path

you must gather
your wits and go
forward in a new
imposition of scale

as you climb the slope
mountain after mountain
appears on the horizon
flowers of altitude
they were waiting
there for you to come
among them
to look across at them
from your own height

what you feel
you can contain
what you see
you will become

the way is upward
through exhaustion
a scree of resistances

glittering muscovite
or white mica
little silver
sparks of sensation

along an arch
or anticline
the rocks lifted
and folded over
in inverse order

the lone violet
of altitude
finds shelter

scramble up
to the ridge
and look over

from complex
negotiations
to vistas
desolations

you are the first
thing the wind meets
as it whistles up
the side of the mountain

rocks, trees
mountains
solitary persons
swept up
in the wind

slopes of sunlight
slopes of snow
sit together
above the scree
innocent
of incident

on the mountain's shoulder
sit on a rocking boulder
rocking and hugging yourself

as you look out
over the hill shapes
you feel your way
over the hill shapes
your eyes walk
over the slopes

looking at hills
you are free of concern
filled with distances
volumes

where enquiry
hurries on
the hill shapes
take their time

take your time
the rise and the swell
of the hills are yours
their weight and implication
rest and aspiration

the hundred
thousand places
with a stone
and some grasses

the dwellings
in ruins
the stones
given back

all the little knots
of anxiety and tension
slowly unravelling
of affection and disaffection
slowly unravelling
the dried grasses trembling

if you move
lightly
events will start
up from your feet

crossing a moor
you are separate
pushed out from
the curve of the hill
or leaning against it

neither moor nor sky
including a sullen
sky and moor
you are broad
and resilient

butterwort
flower of the moor
purple flower
of emptiness

a basal rosette
of carnivorous leaves
the flower single
on a slender stalk

waiting
in emptiness

not the wisp of a breeze
in the lee of the day
among dapples and sedges
rushes and eddies
your pace slackens by
the loch of delay

a forlorn water
do not speak
your name here

a breath is enough
to fan the ripples
of water that run
deliciously in
around dwarf juniper

in the heat of noon
the cool of a pine wood
is refreshing
for man and deer

the songs of shade
are clear songs
thrilling through
gusts of cold

in the gloom the eye
flies to light
to light on a branch
and pause

among shadows
and half-lights
taking place
in their place
the deer
modest
and gratuitous

in a present
they do not
present to themselves
among trees
shedding
their predicates

let them
be there
in the shadows
let them be

who is it
in the pine wood
neither you
nor me

sheltered
the one who
sought shelter
dissolves

a stone from shade
carried for a mile
cool in the hand

there may be a hill
behind a hill
that will invite the gaze
to linger

grey-green behind grey
in looking you are there
it is all you require
this shape this colour

a steep-sided glen
you go on and on
deeper into green
led by implication

you are not where
you are but there
ahead of the given
in continual revelation

knee-deep in bracken
wade out into green
the displaced waves
of bracken fronds
settling around you

as you go forward
you are drawn
forward

green forms
rise up
in front of you

pouring into the visible
as if from some
invisible source

the colours glow
in and around you
you grasp or discard
relations and forms

what is at hand
supports or projects you
you have a mind to
green and gold

a common idiom
carries through
complex articulations
call it a place

it was not your
intention to bring
all your resources
here but you do

a hanging valley
of ash, wych elm, hazel
willow, birch, oak

dense cover of beech
light shade of ash

wintergreen, ramsons
sweet woodruff
guelder rose

hair moss, bracken
fork moss, oak fern
reindeer moss

under a tree
beside a stream
on top of a rock
habitats, dispositions

stands of pine
glades of bracken
ravines of filmy fern
thickets of bog myrtle

birch sapling curving
slightly twisting
out from the slope
rising and turning
in what might
be called a gesture
if a gesture can be
prolonged indefinitely

a breeze
of small birds
moving through
birch leaves

glen of the stones
moss growing over them
trees breaking through them
no path or direction
without plan or intention
you move among stones

to the left, a stone
a stone behind you
beside you a stone
about shoulder height
with moss-covered ledges
ridges and ravines

put your hand
on the hollow rock
place your hollow
hand on the rock

rocks fallen
from high places
keep their composure

you will have to go
all round it
to see it

have to stay
with it
to know it

far down
through green
a drone
of water

a green boat
by a hut
under alders
looking out

the path turns

don't follow it
wait to feel
the lure of it

turning you catch
sight of your own
shadow projected
on green

lured farther
deeper
you are immersed
in green

rising through
leaves and shadows
the imputed
form of the trunk

the attributes
held by
the attribution

the air is cooler
above the stream
that runs through mosses
under the pines

bright slope
of bracken
blue hollow
of bluebells

sit in a debris
of storm damage
thoughtless
in the sunlight

dusty little
butterfly
as if faded
by light

it has taken half a lifetime
to learn to sit in the sun
among primroses and violets
beside a dried adder skin
your back to a broken wall

the grey mare stands
with her back to the rain
tail and mane blown forward
a lean form in a field
facing towards mountains

coming down the hill
you are tall
take it easy
lean back
against the slope

the places
you have been
come with you
you bring experience
to evening air

cattle wade out
into the cool loch margins
among drifts of marsh marigolds
water-mint and speedwell
to stand and bellow
at the setting sun

you will need to know
who you are, to walk
by the solemn lochs

you will have to take on
the volume of a cloud
to move with circumspection

you will need to wear
boots of lead, to walk
by the solemn lochs

in a corner
of a field
unattended
a bonfire
consumes light

by the roadside
a wood
carpeted with wintergreen
wind in the high branches
stillness over moss

before you came here
was there dancing
and are the lugubrious
elders of the wood
pausing

the hill that was bright
is now dark
imperceptibly sensation
glows to emotion
then fades again

there is a faculty
that takes to the moor
and another that brings
you down to the shore

a part of you sheltered
by a gable wall
a part of you open
to the elements

a part of you substantial
and weathered as rock
a part of you mist
dusk and smoke

by an old mooring
a few steps
carved out of rock
go down to water

as if you might
step down into the sea
into another knowledge
wild and cold

far out in the dusk
where qualities mingle
a figure is standing
at the tide's edge

YELLOW & BLUE

on a morning early
when no one
is around
the scree slope
tumbles into
the green lochan

it happens
casually
in the light
available
on a path
that leads
away from it

the truthful ones
the sea-rocks
the skerries
rise from rough waters
into veracity
breaker of boats

skerry of the sea-bent
skerry of the dulse
the yellow skerry
skerry of the strife
to name the rocks
is to navigate
successfully among them
the sparkling skerries
skerry of the anchor
skerry of the deer
landing place of the swan

a tantrum or gale
threw rocks at the gable
tore out the garden
that sat above the sea
in lovely ferocity
poured over breakwaters
piled up plastic
against the blue door

it is a new place
this morning strange
in a light that knows
nothing of the old place
that stood intact
on a bright morning
before the storm

on rocks by the shore
a sheepdog is barking
to round up the waves
but the silly waves
break

speed of the running wave
composure of the standing wave
wit of the rippling wave
delight of the breaking wave

in a wilderness
or bewilderment
of sandwort
and bladder-wrack
small shell place
sheltered

lying back
in the marram grass
out of the wind
listening to the wind
one degree of separation
delivers the sound

there is nowhere to go
there is nothing to do
what would it be
to go somewhere
to do something
who would it be

cumulus nimbus stratus
sandstone basalt granite

it appears the moment
it is mentioned
the hill of bog-cotton
appears and disappears

the residue
of the dissolution
of being
together
huddles
in desolation
by a lonely shore

anything added
may be subtracted
forms half remembered
drift and snag
on jagged
truncated forms
quickly redescribed

when clouds lift
from misty poetry
to see
is to be enlarged
by a faculty

the peeling
birch bark
has a radiant
fringe of light

kitchen midden refuse
ashes bones limpet shells
fragments of pottery
a bit of pumice
a nodule of flint
the hilt with crossguard
of a much-corroded sword

on the cliff edge
the remnant of a net
has blown to cling
to a teasel head
torn blue windflower

flowering gorse bush
leaning over
towards the sea
as if its growth
were towards completion
of yellow in blue

as leaves have grown
back on branches
songs have come
among the leaves
a gathering
in the young
whitebeam

when one thing is tied
loosely to another
the rope drips
dew and sea water
the blue rope
dips in water
then tightens

everything
seems full
until need
fills it

an island across a strand
unapproachable approachable
unapproachable

an island defended by a wall
long ago breached by
ragwort and mountain ash

an island washed away
its lambs at pasture
under the sea

vision leads the mind
beyond islands to a light
or supplement of possibility

some negative features
cut into glacial till
reveal structural elements
a hearth and post holes
a rammed stone floor
extending to a wall
of neatly laid courses
by a threshold stone

sheep and cattle and pigs and goats
saithe and cod and crabs and hens
oats and flax and chert and flint
wood and bone and stone and iron

the vague line of a wall
may be no more than
a fortuitous arrangement
of broken stones
but where it has disappeared
a wall should be inferred
the fort of stillness
continually remade

from speed and noise
a strategic withdrawal
from conformity and self-interest
an abstention
from conspicuous consumption
an absolute retreat

against change it defends itself
against difference it defends itself
against trust it defends itself
against peace it defends itself
against doubt it defends itself

centuries of rain
onslaughts of heat and cold
loosened the structure
loss of authority
the need to stand unguarded
brought it down

in stillness the hills
bulabhal chaipabhal
bolabhal bleabhal
are resting bells
then a wind blows
chaipabhal bolabhal
bulabhal bleabhal
through the syllables

in a high slow turning of gulls
gliding and hanging
dropping and rising
joy samples its levels

the news is news
at the bus stop
in the rain
it is always the same
distant wars
the cleared land
forgotten

the morning bleak
a line of moles
hung on a wire
the burn swollen
bones picked clean

their faces are red
not from shame
but from the wind
from exposure
to their own
waywardness
big red men
striding in an innocence
regained

they go along streets
through doors
into company
airs about them
bare faced

he fell to the floor
people say
but the floor is a ground
not constructed
but given
unconditionally

drinking and falling
down on the earth
getting up and drinking
drinking and falling
down on the earth
getting up and drinking

what excuse to arrive
at an age and feel
preliminary
still raw
the tired strategies
of no avail
only error allowing
access to the real

there are flowers
in the window
of the house collapsing
into the sea
blue flowers

it is fitting to stand
longest by graves
marked only with
an uncarved stone
inserted roughly
into the earth
on a mound of grass
surrounded by a harvest
of gold by the sea

father brother friend
loving husband
wife of the above
relations set in stone
a man and his daughters
a mother and her sons
ragwort round them
the sea near them
grass over them

roots of silverweed
leaves of nettles
fear of eviction

it looks as if the ragwort
grew up in response
to a splash of yellow paint
on a fence post

some quite ordinary
but necessary thing
sunlight or kindness
or the need to be known
recognised in its absence

as if all momentum
came to resolution
hills run to the sea
green sits beside blue
today it might be true
in a light that holds it
steady for inspection

the green by the blue
the blue by the green
keep their values
as keenly as if
the green for the blue
the blue for the green

boys and girls go barefoot
over the machair
through the bentgrass
through the barley
run barefoot everywhere
daylight leads them
in clover in pursuit

in an old inequality
tenacity
of the weed in the soil
fragility
of the crop in the soil

lovely the wave
through the standing barley
a friend of pleasure
would linger
at its edge

a plane of consistency
evenly unfolding
is broken up
by brightness into
bright occasions
that dance a jig
the reel with the burl
the work of the weavers
the morning dew

brightness scatters
any assurance
of being there
there is no
where to place
the increments

something chanced on
a diversion or treasure
that the eye lights on
thought delights in
having form and colour
weight and texture
a word or wonder

in support of
on the side of
in the direction of
an inclination
in italic
for

through clay, sand and gravel
deposited by ice
as glacial drift
acid and impermeable
old peat roads lead
to bogs of sphagnum
cottongrass and deergrass
cloudberry and crowberry

on the open hill
in granite debris
are crystals
of feldspar and mica
the word gems
blue topaz
green beryl
smoky quartz

veins in gneiss
vitreous or resinous
grow geodes
or prismatic crystals
translucent yellow
hard yet ductile
of good cleavage
irregular fracture
almost always
fluorescent

a bed of calcareous rock
drilled blasted screened washed
is transported by water
to aid in the manufacture
of silicon carbide abrasives
leaving an open scar

a deserted or solitary place
desert or inner poverty
emptiness with a clump of grass
an unacres
mere lateral spread or tract

anything that arrives
interrupts a waiting
for the collapse
of expectation
it all starts up again

an insult
hurled in the face
a pebble-dash
of raindrops

on the flushed grassland
cushions of moss campion
green cyphel flowers
white alpine mouse-ear
on the slopes of corries
saxifrage and mountain pansy
take constant nourishment
from soil movement
silting of mountain rills

call it a moor
where thought is under
constant scrutiny
the view from nowhere
a brightness bristling
with thistles

under bird paths
paths of desire
take advantage of
old coffin paths
to rest by cairns
on their way down
to paths across
a mercantile sea

the spirit learns vagueness
from cloud and wool
its density loosening
clinging to wire
twisting and dispersing

the rain-drenched
cloudberries
taste of earth
and cloud

forms of availability
detachment lightness
transparency
bring the gift of the modes
of sympathy
to be able to wait
to move without obstruction
to see far

on crags and slopes
at altitude
on unstable soil
the alpine gentian
gentiana novalis
rare and local

from the crag of the stranger
grey screes fall sheer
to the green lochan
a level of pure
scree-filtered water

fallen from a height
a boulder retains
mass weight position dignity
or acquires them
in its fallen state

leeches in the shallows
of the green lochan
wait to latch on to
a passing affection
black leeches

light grey and deep grey
threaten and lure
soft grey builds distances
in finer shades of grey
cross-hatchings and scumbles
dark grey passes over

looking through greys
to blue and green
the intervening tones
give focus

rain is falling
there and here
on an earth
or ground
repeatedly affirmed
as if it were
unbelievable

too impetuous to be
anywhere
the burn rushes through
the sounds
it throws
in the air

stand sideways to the wind
or hunkering down
present the least
surface to the rain
sit it out or go on
in weather be there
or disappear

the sun comes out
and the sky clears
as decisively as if
a word had been spoken
to launch the great
cattle raid on perception

after a long walk in
to step up to the sky
is exhilarating
if only for
a moment by the cairn
before heading down

on a mountain top
the world spins
when it slows
to a stop
it leans

when the wind drops
calm is free
of predicates
a thorn
stripped of blossom

little crystals
in the ear
adjust to
pressure
as the earth tilts
over

at its upper limit
the mountain pansy
viola lutea
rooted in uncertainty
is blue and yellow
briefly

to remember it
is to visit it
again in thought
to lean
closer in
briefly

glamour stands scrutiny
the world is sonorous
spacious and chromatic
fragrant, formidable
responding to the touch

lie back in the heather
the winds are silk
cloths drawn lightly
over the slopes
the cheek bones

a basket woven
with goldenrod
and marjoram
heavy with apples
is not more welcome
than a glen that sweeps
up nothing in its arms
to offer it
for delectation

whatever is touched
steps back
the impossible flower
the immediate
at arm's length
under the fingertips

many discursive influences
pour into the argument
of a mountain burn
in a pedantry that runs on
while sense traverses it
delight rushes through it

in the din of the waterfall
overtones of bells
in the wind, variation
thrushes tapping shells
hebridean bees
listening beyond themselves
approach quiet by degrees

from turbulence to turbulence
the water fills
a hollow that holds it
still for a while
a turbulence interrupted
the stillness a constant
exchange of water

sylphs and nymphs and kelpies
might slip between
silks and shocks and sulks
of water into real bodies

consonants with varied
points of articulation
palatalised and rounded
sibilants affricates
clicks clacks diphthongs
a burn or babble
of open vowels

roots rocks boulders
stops and labials
gutters and runnels
dentals constrictives

forgetting brings loss
of articulation
the language of the heart
a smoke

stone dressed in water
a smooth or slick
drape of water
moulding its facets

the force
of water stuns
deaf to sense
things stand
astonished

there is a place
of sunlight
under birch trees
separate
across a torrent

lean closer
to the slope
inside
an antique
music trickles
it tickles
the curiosity
of the unwary

older than looking
this listening
older than listening
this lonesome
touch

efficacious songs are never sung
aloud but only under
a splashing of rushing water
aside or athwart
to the silverweed
to primrose to pearlwort

a song of herding
a song of milking
a song of smooring
a song of kindling
words on the breaking
of bread

while water flows
a tune runs contrary
tug of desire
against contingency
that it all stay
nothing be lost
the turbulence least

in an anonymous place
of couch grass and thorns
there is a parting
a lesion
something is given
into the world's keeping

sometimes a name
will be enough to loosen
desire for a while
loch of the stepping stones
no need to go there

everyone
gets soaked
to the skin
except the thin
theorist of rain

sketch of a wild rose
in watercolour
dissolving

a path laid down
in granite
leads up through
the immediate
a green of young
birch leaves
aspen leaves
trembling

on the slope, a wood
of birch and hazel
waking to morning
falls through the light
that falls through it

at an angle of light
the leaves of wild garlic
have a silver sheen
that empties their form
nowhere spreading everywhere
under the trees

as a swarm of wasps
is drawn to a slick
of aphids along
a pine branch
a quality of darkness
under the pines
is attractive

shades of green
lead farther in
to a green that glows
internally
then paths of green
close up again
behind one who passes
lightly

solitaries in community
the pines
at dawn and at dusk
in observance

all the water pouring
over the waterfall
confirms the notion
of a waterfall
the form rests
while the water flows

intelligence nimble
fine webs thrown
across branches
inference over gaps
a squirrel laughs
from high in the tree
at water falling
continually

the path picks up
again on the other
side of a fallen tree
but the intervening
bulk of the trunk
shatters complacency

the broken giants
battered foliage
jagged edges
of the great
raised wounds

to move among
crashing pines
is spacious
and exact

gear and tackle
grapple with lengths
of felled pine
the staggering
tilting weights
set down

it takes a lot
of noise to clear
old sunlight
from pine woods

the ground is a scrub
a complex weaving
or layering of bracken
bilberry and least willow
each step must be
tested carefully
a way found by forsaking
the forgetting of trust

amid storm damage
a debris of quiet
the attacked heart healing
picnic on a log

a pact for peace
a league for peace
a treaty or entreaty
for perpetual peace
a forest
for

light that might
spread indefinitely
never to be known
is trapped in leaves
and pulled down
through the tree canopy
around everybody

layers of branches
ranks of tall grasses
deposits of leaves
turf and mulch
insist on the hatching
of horizontal with vertical
as rich exchange
a constantly occurring
ascending and descending

a wind blown cloud
deepens the shade
or lightens it
by dispersing again
putting in question
the provenance of shade
its stability and spread

in a context of green
the graces dance
in weeds of green
neatly
away from inspection

toys and trinkets
placed in a tree
in recognition
of a mystery
dispersed in
toys and trinkets

one in constant
modulation
may be a tree
a bird a stone
startled
in the light
of recognition

or
the golden word
ripple of variation
lever of possibility
an oar

stone into gold
gold into stone
wheat into bread
desire to fruition
gravity to levity
dependency to autonomy
sorrow into yarrow
water into melody

year after year
it builds its nest
of twigs and grass
mud and moss
where anyone
might find it

shape shade
nuance tone
words that go in
under round
by thorn light
often torn

at a tap
a cloud
of pollen
spills
to drift
in a puff
of dust

in the light-filled wood
a wall a lintel some stairs
as if the parings of a life
were preserved in honey jars

something discrete
is led to
discretion
as if taken
by the hand

in the wood in the fall
in the woolly heads
of willow herb
a chapel in ruins

when the light shifts
countless trembling
raindrops on birch twigs
fade to a clarity that seems
the temper of the day
until light returns
to the shining tree

when a breeze blows
through grasses or branches
light touches the harp
there are no witnesses
only musicians, dancers

yellow in shade
is a modified green
cool and contained
not seeking the light
but allowing a dappled
light to find it

at the edge of shadow
a drift of speedwell
makes a pool of blue
a transition to brightness
casting retrospective
haze over shadows

if the light of the sun
is focused through a lens
it will burn
intently
giving off smoke
leaving a dark
mark of intention
sunlight on wood

after rain
briar leaves
have a scent
of apples

starting over there
and coming back
all the way across
intervening distance
where might
enquiry end

springs and wells are doors
doors are springs and wells

here is a garden
of tansy run riot
around anyone
bright enough
to neglect it

the lintel is broken
four walls still stand
sheep occupy an absence
of the well-spoken
habit of the house

nothing hides
in the abandoned places
no household gods
no folded spaces
flint left in the wall
long idle

three milking cows
tethered in the byre
hens in and out
at the scullery window
bread and cream
blue and white ware
eggs in the straw
the clock ticking

in a back parlour
the best furniture
is seldom used
linen is folded
neatly in a drawer
fresh for an occasion
that never arrives
the clock ticking

a jug of water
a chink of light
a twist of smoke

step closer
someone is there
in the shadows
looking out

by a window
blue cornflowers
in a yellow cup
continually
wake up

cleanse and thicken the cloth
by beating after weaving
rhythmically beating and singing
cleanse and thicken and soften the cloth
by soaking it and thumping it
in company in time
waulking the newly woven cloth

wash it in the burn
dry it on a thorn
sew it with a needle
with pure white thread
putting the iron on it
press it and warm it
place it crisp and folded
in the right hands

the wells and the burns
the fruits of labour
the moor and the machair
the stories and tunes
a quality of welcome
the spaces of custom
of communal negotiation
brought under authority
of gentry and clergy

rent is in kind
oats barley
wethers chickens
with a right to gather
wind scattered wits
heather and peat
on the heart slope
in the rain

before darkening
the threshold
be sure to bring
straws of brightness
shards of cold air
into company

or bring nothing
on a visit
nothing to divert
the gasp
of welcome

the crofter a weaver
the postman a baker
the fisherman a shepherd
the poet a mender of roads

a stone picked up
a weight set down
a role assumed
or discarded

neighbours on the doorstep
nomads at a border

twisting heather twigs
twining quicken roots
plaiting bentgrass
in peat reek
spinning and carding
scolding and teasing
knitting and darning
out of the sleet

bending down
by the burn
to pick fresh
water mint
did they pause
for a moment
out of the wind

woven with hazel and willow
with hazel and willow woven
woven with hazel and willow
with hazel and willow woven
woven with hazel and willow

let this
trouble pass
to a trick
or a turn
at a word
let it swerve
past

hold the bucket
under water until
the bucket fills up
then carry the bucket
up the slope careful
not to spill a drop

forgetting is a second clearance
attention to distance
loss of the near at hand

what will become of us
here on the edge
in the bitter wind
on acid soil
beside the waiting
transports

there were bridles of grasses
pulled from the machair
on the gentle horses
riding into war

a basket left
among the grasses
is soon claimed
by the grasses

how lovely now
is the fluttering
of a yellow butterfly
in the margins
of my book

warmth from the straw
draws the dew
into a hollow lined
with straw and clay
worked into a puddle
trampled by cattle
it will hold water
a cool place at noon
the dew pond

in mist filled hollows
gravity extracts
moisture from air
in the cloud pond
the fog pond
the frog pond
the dew pond

tall blind grasses
ripple in a breeze
that breathes through them
a hand brushes over them
the many-coloured grasses
knowing nothing of colour
seed in a haze
nothing rooted sees

to come down
to the shelter
of a sunlit hollow
is to step
into a warmth
of reception

nothing is deeper
than a surface of water
sipped by swallows
the slight
truth of shallows
support of lilies

across the level
expanse of the lochan
point instants of rain
hardly remain
for long enough
to register
here and there
there and here

flowers rare
leaves light green
floating on water
lemna minor
small green ovals
drifting in shoals
in ditches and pools

the negative space
of the lochan
replaces earth with sky
a gap in pure extension
it is an overturning
of the reasonable
the dry

when ducks push through
duckweed it floats
in again behind them

on the fiddler's path
along the river
notes play over
notes of water
in a continuous stream of sound
the waulking of the plaiding
daft robin
a slow air

thrushes take the tune
and all the family
of hedges and distances
answer in antiphony

the blackbird in the hedge
warbler on a thorn
thrush of the afternoon
sweeter their notes than bells
harps or accordions

aside from the path
the anti-fiddler
scrapes away
at nothing
picking and unpicking
the plaid of sense
in a farewell to whisky
a slow air

sanding it down
paring it down
the rind
the integument
diluting it
thinning it
the defining line
the boundary

in the heat of afternoon
quiet suffers reduction
to a one stone drone
a latent power
dangerous to strangers

if shade were shelter
for things from their names
the young bull might sit
in imageless absorption
its ferocity cooling

willow branches lift and fall
and in falling seem to slow
to lag behind an inference
of the course of respiring branches
an image settling like snow

the hill that was dark
is now bright
imperceptibly sensation
glows to emotion
then fades again

it flaps away
the lapwing
it claps away
laps away
away

the scent of meadowsweet
a memory of the scent
of meadowsweet

impetuous
little flurry
of raindrops
on the brushed
snare drum
of the pond

to go on and on
to have more of the same
is the one desire
of the solitary walker
in the just intonation
of the river meadow
in late afternoon

arcs and loops and angles
long leisurely
flights of abstraction
of lines over water
settle on water
sedge on the evening rise

the land of twilight
of the sunset
the west
a land of evening
of a levelling
prolonged

the weaving of grasses dust
dust the weaver of grasses

far out on the lochan
two red-throated divers
drift on the water
this way and that
in a lack of volition
given to the water
turning together
this way and that

if you were mine
I would hold you
if you were mine
I would rock you
if you were mine
I would lift you
over the stile
into morning

little muntjack deer
running through the corn
in flight from form
in the gloaming

preserve us from calm
that brings in the night
harm to islands

a lamp of fish oil
with a wick of rushes
gathered by the light
of the full moon

FARM BY THE SHORE

sea separates from sky
earth from sea
all things take shape
from darkness

do you know the land
where bog cotton grows

on the littoral
among the laminarias
at the equinoctial
low spring tide
the tonality or ethos
of a floating world
is pooled in rock
in wrack and tangle

nothing is lovelier
than the grey line
that approaches and departs
from precision

in the truce of the morning
the bitter taste
of the memory of talk
a debris in the wake
of eagerness

green floats in the mist and haze
then green floats in the haze
then green floats

for the nurture
of all things is moist
warmth itself coming
to be from the moist
the seeds of all things
being moist in nature

an island balanced on a line of light
a ship sailing through the sky

a blue bird
that makes its nest
on a calm sea
and in the woven
water lays
three blue eggs

before the coming of snow
long strings of deer
make their way down the hillside
the straths fill with them
as the mind is full
at the thought of them
before the coming of snow

don't flinch away
let the wind slice through
defensive attitudes
connective tissue
ramparts of the hill fort

high snow slopes
sweetened by wind
touch blue
to draw the eye
to cornices
brushstrokes

glittering in gneiss
snowflakes on eyelashes
frail songs by torrents

in reduced visibility
going is staying
in the little territory

it would seem
to be the sum
of perceptions
for what is not
perceived is not

each time sing a long tone
into the drone of the wind
then adjust it up or down
closer to the drone of the wind

between stimulus and response
the grey lag

stratus cumulus nimbus
where you look you go
cirrus altostratus

perceptions are dew
people are mist
days are thistledown

everything melts
but the snow is sheltered
for a while by a wall

as yet some part
of your mind
is limestone
skeletons of coral
petrified crinoid
feeling welling up

so dark in the well
so clear in the light
so sweet on the lips
so cold in the throat

it takes all the mass
and momentum
of a mountain
to intimidate its own
contingency

if it comes towards you
at the exact speed
as you go towards it
in expectation
get out of the way

climbing up onto
the mountain's shoulder
you step above yourself
to be among mountains
that stand around in the cold

a stone from the shore
carried in the rucksack
to act as a ballast
to the impetus of summits

on a clear day
while the mountains
turn in a dance
to a reel
or slip jig
join in the mad
mountain dance

by the rush of a torrent
in the din of the flow
listen to tighten
the strings of the harp

but come consider
how each thing is
presented to trust
to sight or taste
to thought or touch

for there are these alone
pouring through one another
dallying with one another
intermingling
the hot the cold the wet the dry
in motion change and time
coming together and parting
for shapes never tire of shifting

yellow shines through the mist and haze
then yellow shines through the haze
then yellow shines

here are waterfalls
that flow upward
hills that dip
their heads in pools
roads that idle
in sorrel

if you have to sail
through a storm to reach it
or trek into it
knee-deep through a bog
it's not nature
if you need to inspect it
through a microscope
on a cold day
hanging from a cliff

a summer walker
you climbed no higher
than the lower slopes
delayed by blaeberries
and lack of ambition

the trust of the first
celandines opening
the first of the trust

between gorse and coltsfoot
the yellowhammer
between coltsfoot and gorse

anyone who comes
to yellow wants
more

a prodigality of skylarks
a liberality of skylarks
a virtuosity of skylarks
a spontaneity of skylarks

you could be
extravagantly
straightforward
you might be
categorically
at ease

crocuses crowding
thick on the bank
in clusters under trees
build to a chorus
as the colour fills

a long tendril
to twist and twine
a tender intuition
at the end of the stem
allows the tufted vetch
to cling and climb
to clamber
over the hedge

quicker than tadpoles
in pools the shadows
of tadpoles in pools
or the notion of shadows
of tadpoles in pools

the wren has entered
an exacting freedom
within the thicket
of prepositions

the stone
in your hand
is a shape
in your hand
the weight
in your hand
is cold

do you feel you must reach
for a separate name
distinct from the grain
beneath your fingers

deposits of sediments
longshore drift
plate tectonics
sleep in the afternoon

born from thunder
damsel fly

the force or inertia
that brought the boulder
to lodge against the birch
is irreducible

a man bending over a pool
reaching in to take
something from the pool
takes something
from the pool

many a good man
sings to himself

much that is light
outshines itself
dazed in a grace
that comes to it
as unimpeded movement
it throws a thought
and catches it
farther on

not as a stranger
you move surely
through the lonely places
surely not a stranger

familiar of the salt marsh
of the dune slack the machair
familiar with the pasture
the set aside

sitting on a rock
having kinship with rock
of one impulse with
waves and wheat

ubiquitous frog noise
loud and harsh joy
of raw altered states
drone with flute and harmonium
scraped singing bowls

distance and proximity
a downhill tumble
proximity and distance
through the downy willow
distance and proximity

there are practices
to augment experience
over-ruling lore
habits that allow
for exception
dispositions that bring
faculties to vision

the term undoes its negation
you pine for what you deny
the shade is deep and fragrant
in a forest without trees

noun intending its object
stoat chasing a rabbit

the weavers of tales
and the spinners of fates
are in collusion

a splash of cold
water on the wrists
you survive
your absences

a thin trickle
of water through
the watercress
is enough

small brown bird throat white
breast suffused with peach
hidden in a glancing light
vanishes when it stops singing

a warbler among the leaves
as if the leaves
had come to the notion
of a warbler among the leaves

by the side of a road
relentless in heat and dust
sycamores store darkness
great reserves of coolness

under the branches
everything dissolves
in coolness
a stillness
spreads through anything
that moves

light builds a darkness
within the tree
to a shock of cold
or transparency

no practice
for shade
but a practice
of shade

they found the shapes in trees
to build the boats to follow
sea lanes to spices

in the graphite shade
the cracked black pepper
grain of the wood
everything drifts

through the long grass
something runs
from predication and assumption
into possibility
almost successfully

complexity is distributed
across the birch scrub
at a glance a movement
is described and redescribed
swiftly across the birch scrub

although the branches are still
they reach out across
the space to other branches
you will see or feel
their branching as reaching
although the branches are still

a turbulence in water
a perturbation of the air
thrills through the wood as cold
or a water song in leaves

a trembling
in the leaves
gathers beyond
its impetus
a commotion
or contagion
in the leaves

as you move through the trees
they shift around you
jostling for position
until everything you see
has sight of you

something only
glimpsed is something
something barely
discerned is something
something hardly
there is something

deer and shade
trunk and torso
nominal distinctions

antlers locked with sunbeams
peeled velvet
moss

things are vibrations
that steady
briefly
their locality
is variable
a continual tending
or tuning
to the place

second
person
singular
or plural

of bodies changed to new shapes
of minds changed
the breeze informs you
the shadows tell you
of garments into foliage
limbs to branches

through the gesture
the impulse
in the gesture
flows
carried to
a liberty
only the gesture
allows

variation is the way of heaven
try on this shape
try on that shape
in mimicry of integrity
approach it

try on this colour
try on that colour
how do they suit
your complexion

dark blue light blue
winter green hunter green
olive mahogany tan
deep mauve dark plum

under the chords and clavichords
of the river in the wood
all the sympathetic
strings sound

wayward impulse
owned by no one
blown moth

a breeze that stirred
a word you heard
shifting the balance

glades in woods unvisited
unvisited glades in woods
glades in words unvisited

how did you get here
your mind wandering
what grace guided your steps

green one of the wood

a place to which
you might retreat
retire or repair
to petition for nuance
perhaps to drop
to sleep a bit
to learned distinctions
a wish for shade
granted

grapes of the north
raindrops

colour is balance
a shade or a tone
something in between
mint and thyme

ovals of light
are sprinkled over
scattered chickweed
wintergreen

here muntjac deer
browse oxlip flowers
leaving the leaves
unbruised

gean and juniper
the small-leaved lime
rowan and alder
take your time

fluttering dove
dove hovering
settling dove

written in shadow
a short history
of delay

propriety might stretch
a dandelion rope
across the trees
giving pause

how it worries
away at conviction
the flicker of everything
at the edge of attention

hart's tongue and adder's spit
fern fronds unfurling
croziers of bladder fern
volutes of bracken
spleenwort and polypody

light beside bracken
light on bracken
light behind bracken

a comma resting
on the path,

on bright days when the wood
is veiled in blue light
light in the wood seems
to be a light of the wood
given out while contained

perhaps the more
need not appear
if it is there
in support
or suggestion
there is more

alder and oak and birch
hawthorn rowan willow
talk to each other again
lime and larch and pine
whitebeam gean hazel

the wound
of the sound
of an axe
in the wood
aches

sons and daughters of early risers
would steal the light from your door
daughters and sons of early risers
on a fine day ask for more

the slopes eroded
the land claimed
the rivers braided
the burns dammed

a volume of coarse-grained sediment
is hurried along a gradient
in a specific gravity of water
until erosion is deposited
in islands and bars separated
by multiple channels or braids
zones of confluence and diffluence

the immediate heirs
of the present holder
each have equal
entitlement to land
everyone gets a share
of wind and rain
of arable and bog
even to ruinous
fragmentation

who knocks
at the door
who stands
on the threshold
who blocks
the light
from the porch

rumour slander innuendo
stick to the names
of far-flung clans
status is a stake
in qualities
transported along rivers
into glens

a plant a herbivore a predator
and a predator of the predator
a space of distribution
and a time of predation

help with the peats
will be given in return for
help with the peats
support is in kind
but reciprocity
has its boundary
sheep may stray

it is better to be battered
by a second cousin
than beaten up
by a neighbour
consanguinity takes precedence
over contiguity
you would rather be throttled
by your mother's brother
than strangled
by a stranger

if you can hide
and not get caught
then run out
and kick the can
you are it

the dry ones
the long thin ones
who leaned in doorways long ago
who rolled their cigarettes in rain
they mould your cheekbones
they fur your arteries

in among the whins
there is a stone
once you could have read
the name on it

go able men
arrayed in most
warlike manner
running in foray
taking kye
oxen horses
gold and money
burning houses
mutilating many
to drink of gentle
blood and free
then ladies woe
shall cry

winds are disconsolate
burns flow circumspectly
birds mourn on the branches
since you have gone

the shapes and colours
have lost their relation
the surfaces miss
your hand on them

not for peace in the gloaming
not for space in the morning
not for silver or gold
will you return

the weaving and unravelling
of fragrant meadow grasses
the braiding and undoing
of hair-moss and willow
the tightening and loosening
of bonds of affection
the stretching and breaking
of long melodic strands
the spinning and extending
of strings of narrative
the twining and twisting
of dogwood and rowan

practice or pattern
according to reason
carried in tradition

a wad of wool
or flax is hooked
to the top of the distaff
then drawn out
towards the spindle
which is spun under
its own momentum
as the earth turns
round the sun

for a smooth yarn
wet the fibre
with your finger
as you spin

fishers for pearls
pine cone gatherers
shy folk
washed from the river bank
faded from the wood

land poor in itself
grazed and burnt
beaten by lashing rain
could regenerate again
to heathland and mire
herb rich grassland
scrub in mosaic

herons by pools
goldfinches at the seed heads
raptors over hills

here is what there is
the sure and present
sense of what there is

thick blanket bog peat

in and on the water on and in

a raft of sphagnum and sedges

anchored in mud or floating free

a buzzard circling under pondweed

the waters of the lochan
fanned by a breeze
run for the cover
of reeds and sedges
rocking the pondweed

as a sylph into silken waters
slip between the clean sheets
of the scent of mown hay

as I me went
by water side
full fast in mind
ran water sound
a lady bright
there gave me leave
to lay down lightly
by her

water that flows
through watercress
receives the qualities
of watercress

lapping of the little
waves at quiet
continual lapping
of the little waves
unquiet on quiet
the first harmonics

in the bud
there is the poise
of possibility
as if pausing
to anticipate
the waterlily

by the lap lapping of the water
the dip dipping of a dipper
in the light dapples over
over water and dipper

clouds among waterlilies
part leaving waterlilies
doubled in reflection
until the clarity clouds

gold leaf laid on water

moonwort milkwort
slender st john's wort
that they might be known
have their time in the sun
lousewort and bitter vetch

anyone who is given
a promise of happiness
should insist that it is
redeemed

ephemera...
food of swallows

what remains is pollen
pine stumps and spores
coleopteran fragments
evidence of clearance
of erosion or acidification
precariously preserved
in archives in bogs

meadows of windloving flowers
ferns and fungi and mosses
produce great quantities
of light-weight grains
of pollen to be distributed
broadly on currents of air

suspended in clouds
fossilised in rocks
hidden in the lint
in a jacket pocket
in furrows and fissures
dirt tracks and ditches

in pool and in hollow
deposits of the pollen
of sycamore and willow
deposits of the pollen
of meadowsweet and mallow
in pool and in hollow

when a warbler lights
on a tall grass
grass and warbler
dip
and right themselves
and swing

the things that mean most
are spoken of least

from
bog
myrtle

when the mare canters
across the meadow
a breeze stirs
the fragrant grasses

softly step
over the boundaries
in sunshine
without fear

brighter than soldiers
in all their armour
is the one you love
coming through clover

wetland and hazel woodland
species-rich grassland
tall herb communities
peat bog and coastal heath

keep the cattle out
let the meadow germinate
flower and seed
then let the cattle in

cut the silage late
after the seed has set
graze tightly in winter
to clean up the pasture

sheep and cattle on the hill
mountain hare in the margins
voles on the in-bye
transparent burnet moth

grass of parnassus
wood bitter vetch
scarce bog orchid
sword-leaved helleborine

lenticular cloud above the headland
a glee-club of goldfinches
the sea blue behind
devil's bit scabious

small oats rye bere barley
ripe harvest in late summer
a shallow ploughing
grazing and fallow in rotation

corncrake and corn bunting
great yellow bumble bee
oystercatcher lapwing golden plover
orchid vetch and clover

when no one is home
the strawberry roan
stands in the rain
forlorn

mattress of heather
of bracken or eelgrass
pillow of cottongrass
stuffed with a down
of coltsfoot or reedmace
floor strewn with bog myrtle

strong rope of heather
honeysuckle bridle
twisted birch bark tether
fish trap of sedge
purple moor-grass anchor rope

scatter rue across the floor
place rue among the linen
blue-leaved bitter-leaved rue
that springs anew
after burial in snow
set a bank of rue
herb of grace
restorer of vision
for there is much to see

open the door and startle a deer

of no particular gifts
having no particular intention
but to while or whittle the time
in ling and tormentil

good for nothing
but for taking
the idle road
to nothing but

the horse in the field is a horse
the word horse is a word
they are both a little hoarse

plenitude of the sensible
going down to the sea
as to a value as sure
as a sense of direction

an appetite for blue
precedes and survives
a quantity of blue
or qualities of grey
of gold or silver

in fidelity to clarity
the wounds in the rocks
open

blue sits beside green
green beside yellow
separately
each is its own
but shines in company

if you tell yourself to look
then to look more intently
you add imperative
to imperative
if you tell yourself to look
then to look less intently

warm light pours out
through the open door
but the door is too low
to give access

the well of virtues
how is it far

shells and pebbles
rags of linen
stuffs worn out
offered in tribute
pins and needles
rusty nails

the grove of delight
you are almost
there

go down to the boat
come to it
through the wet grass
against the slight
weight
of the wet grass

three knots in a rope
if you run into a storm
untie the first knot
if you run into a storm
untie the second knot
never untie the third knot

bird with a call
like a comb scraped
against a credit card
on tip toe go
through the hay ho
who will know

success is in excess
of the aspiration
it is a disappointment
sad horses stand
in gathering dusk
beside the ploughed field

smoke and wool snagged on wire
old stories told through smoke
smoke from burning carried away
scent of crushed rosemary and smoke
smoke screen of old stories
a theft of honey in a puff of smoke

wrap your blanket
of mist and cloud
woven of waiting
around me
my love

the grasses are flowering
the bracken is turning
the swallows are gathering

when you see the direction
of the melody
your fingers will follow
across the strings

fine lines of fracture
mended with gold

the cattle take
the same road
at the same time
every day
turn in
at the same gate
towards evening

as light fades from the hills
feeling pervades the fields
they are not at rest
while the light lasts

a mountain in mist and rain
you went there and returned
you are not the same

around sprigs of lavender
along the stems of sea holly
it is already evening

a child might take you
by the hand and lead you
to dusk at the wood's edge

sitting in the dusk
duration becomes substance
you could lay your hand on it

who knows where
the light ends
or the resonance
of the bell stops

the black stone from the shore
here it is on the black table

magick moonwort or honesty
dried peeled oval seedpods
little transparent hanging moons
or satin silver dollars
may be used to gather moonlit dew

the sound of the sea in your head
in the bed by the window
in the moonlight on the tide
on the pillow of a wave

your name is not heard
in the reeds by the lochan
where once the rocks
threw it back

a small fragment
of a golden sickle
dug out of moss